Welcome to FORTY, a brand new collection of delicious fish and shellfish recipes to celebrate 40 years of Ramus Seafoods. Inside you'll find nutritious family favourites and simple suppers as well as exciting ideas for entertaining. We're fortunate to have recipes from many acclaimed chefs, food writers and local restaurants alongside our own, so there'll be plenty to inspire you.

Responsible sourcing of our products is very important to us at Ramus and we are proud to support the Fishermen's Mission charity, with a donation from every book going to help those who catch our fabulous fish.

Nothing can beat the great taste of fresh seafood cooked simply, and through FORTY we hope to inspire you to reap the benefits of the ultimate fast food.

THE FISHERMEN'S MISSION

'Providing a lifeline of welfare and support to fishermen and their families'

HERE ARE SOME WORDS ABOUT US!

The Fishermen's Mission (also known as the Royal National Mission to Deep Sea Fishermen) is the only national charity that works solely to offer support to active and retired fishermen and their families. We do this by offering practical, financial and pastoral support as well as offering a 24 hour emergency service to injured or sick fishermen at sea. Since 1881 we have been working to help our brave fishermen who go out to sea to bring home their catch and also their families who wait for them to return safely home.

www.fishermensmission.org.uk

CONTENTS

Our Story .... **4 – 7**

Shellfish Recipes .... **8 – 27**

How to... Shellfish	10 – 11	Mussels	20 – 22
Crab	12 – 14	Clam	23 – 23
Scallops	15 – 17	Prawns	24 – 25
Lobster	18 – 19	Squid	26 – 27

Fish Recipes .... **28 – 67**

How to... Fish	30 – 33	Flat Fish	52 – 55
White Fish	34 – 51	Oily Fish	56 – 67

Our Catch .... **68 – 79**

Contributors **80**

OUR STORY

From humble beginnings supplying Scottish lobster to Harrogate hotels, to the accolades of being the number one importer of Canadian lobster and Independent Seafood Retailer of the Year, Ramus has built up a trusted reputation for fabulous quality, personal customer service and great value.

Established by Chris and Liz Ramus in 1974, Ramus opened the doors of its first shop on Otley Road, Harrogate in 1975. Building on the valuable experience gained in his father's butchery business, Chris saw a gap in the market for supplying fresh quality seafood to the county's best restaurants.

1974

Kings Road, Harrogate

With its reputation building and Harrogate clamouring for Ramus's fresh fish and lobster, the company moved to new premises on Kings Road in 1983. Complete with retail shop, a state of the art processing plant and huge seawater lobster tanks, Ramus could now supply fresh quality fish across Yorkshire and beyond.

Securing The Future

In 1999 Ramus moved from a partnership to a limited company, with directors Jonathan Batchelor and Tony Rushton taking a share of the company and securing its future. With over 50 cumulative years in the business, their knowledge and experience is second to none.

1983

1999

The first Ramus Seafood Emporium

October 2000 saw the grand opening of the first Ramus Seafood Emporium on Kings Road, Harrogate. With its huge range of products and complementary items, they were able to supply both their loyal Harrogate customers as well as many of the finest restaurants and professional kitchens in the area.

Seafood Retailer of the Year

In 2005 Ramus won the coveted Independent Seafood Retailer of the Year, awarded by the industry body Seafish, for excellence in fishmongery. These awards have not been run for many years but customers trust Ramus to still perform at the highest national standards.

2000

2005

Opening our Doors in Ilkley

Ilkley was the next logical step for Ramus in their aim to broaden the supply of fine fresh fish and seafood. Opening in 2007 to great acclaim, their shop in Victorian Mews showcased the delights of Ramus to the rest of the Dales.

Forty Years

2014 is the most exciting year yet, with Ramus celebrating 40 years in the business. Not only have the stores been refitted to include delicious complementary products and wine but a brand new recipe book has been released, full of top tips, advice and inspiration.

2007

2014

SHELLFISH RECIPES

8 - 27

———— FISH FACT ————

The collective name for a group of
crabs is a 'cast' and baby crabs are
known as hatchlings.

HOW TO...
DRESS A LOBSTER

1. Pull off claws and set to one side.

2. Insert sharp, stiff knife into back of lobster and cut down middle towards head.

3. Turn it around and cut towards the tail, keeping tail tucked underneath & splitting into 2 equal halves. Remove head cavity and intestinal tract from each half of lobster.

4. Using back of knife, crack claws to expose meat, leaving claw half of shell intact. Extract meat from remaining knuckles and use to fill any empty shell space.

HOW TO...
DRESS A CRAB

1. Pull shell away from body and legs. Remove skull, stomach sac and feathery dead men's fingers.

2. Remove all brown meat from inside head. Crack & trim edges of crab shell for neat presentation. Chop brown meat and place back into prepared shell.

3. Remove large claws & extract meat from remaining legs & body (make sure all 'dead men's fingers' are discarded).

4. There is plenty of white meat inside the body, small legs & knuckles – use a lobster pick to extract as much as possible. Crack claws in same way as lobster.

5. Place white meat on top of brown inside shell, displaying claws on either side.

11

Created by Jonathan Batchelor, Ramus

POTTED CRAB TARTLETS

Makes 24 tartlets

454g hand-picked white crabmeat
24 tartlet cases
½ green and ½ red chilli, diced

Zest of 1 lemon, juice of ½ lemon
Freshly ground nutmeg, pinch
Clarified butter *(made with 250g pack)*
Chopped dill
Salt and pepper

METHOD – To make the clarified butter, put 250g unsalted butter, cut into chunks, into a saucepan on a low heat until melted. Skim off any scum, then leave to stand until separated. Use a ladle to take off the clear clarified butter, leaving the milk solids behind. Store until required.

Bake off the pastry cases as per the instructions. Mix the white crabmeat, chillies, lemon zest, and nutmeg together in a bowl.

Add 1 tbsp clarified butter and mix together. Spoon the mix into your tartlet cases and press down the mix to leave a good space between the mix and the top of the case.

Pour enough clarified butter into each tartlet to cover the crab mix. Garnish with some finely chopped dill and refrigerate for an hour to set.

TOP TIP – Clarified butter has a higher smoke point than butter, meaning that it doesn't burn so easily. It is therefore particularly good for pan frying fish. Once made, it can be stored in the fridge for months or in an airtight container for a few weeks.

WINE MATCH – Try a Sauvignon Gris or
New World Sauvignon Blanc.

CRAB PITHIVIERS

Serves Four

200g fresh, white crab meat,
squeezed dry
55g unsalted butter
2 shallots, peeled and chopped
1 carrot, peeled and grated

25g white breadcrumbs
Salt and pepper
750g puff pastry, chilled
1 whole egg and 1 egg yolk
(beaten together)
4 tsp sour cream
Handful fresh coriander

METHOD – Begin by preparing the filling. In a large frying pan, melt the butter over a medium heat. Add the finely chopped shallots and grated carrot and cook gently for approx 5 minutes. Do not let the mixture colour, lower the heat if this starts to happen.

After 5 mins, add the crab and cook for a further minute. Remove the pan from the heat and add the breadcrumbs. Mix well and season to taste with a little salt and pepper and put to one side to cool completely.

Roll out the pastry to the thickness of a pound coin. Then either cut 4 x 10cm circles and 4 x 12 cm circles (if you want to make individual Pithiviers) or, cut two circles of pastry approx 24 cm and 26 cm for one large Pithivier. Brush the smaller circles of pastry with the beaten egg mixture.

If making individual tarts, divide the cold crab meat mixture into four and place one portion onto each of the smaller circles. Sprinkle over fresh coriander. Make a small well in the centre of the filling and fill with soured cream. Place the larger piece of pastry over the first, press around the edges. Freeze for twenty minutes, or wrap and freeze until required.

When you are ready to cook the Pithiviers preheat the oven to 180°C. Remove the Pithiviers from the freezer, cut a small round from the centre of each Pithiviers, this is to allow any steam to escape during cooking. Using a sharp knife, score a curved pattern into the top of the pastry taking care not to cut right through! Glaze the pie with the beaten egg.

For the individual Pithiviers, cook in the preheated oven for 12-15 minutes (20-25 minutes for the large size) or until golden brown and well risen. Serve immediately.

SCALLOPS IN A WHITE WINE SAUCE WITH WATERCRESS

Serves Four

30g ground turmeric
30g plain flour
12 large scallops, shelled, corals removed, washed and dried
2 tbsp oil
140g unsalted butter, cubed

Sea salt and ground black pepper
1 shallot, finely chopped
175ml dry sparkling white wine
140ml fish stock
140ml chicken stock
140ml double cream
Large bunch watercress, *(leaves only)*
Freshly grated nutmeg

METHOD – Mix the turmeric and flour together in a bowl. Dip one side of the scallops in the mixture and shake off any excess. Heat the oil in a frying pan over a high heat. Add 30g butter. When melted, cook the scallops floured-side down for 1-2 minutes or until golden-brown.

Turn over the scallops and season with a little salt. Cook until just coloured (about 30 seconds to a minute), then remove from the pan and keep warm.

Drain half the fat from the pan, add the shallot and fry gently until soft but not coloured. Add the wine and bring to the boil. Cook until the volume of liquid has reduced by two-thirds. Add the stocks and reduce again by half. Add the cream and reduce to a sauce consistency. Season with salt and freshly ground black pepper. Beat in 80g butter until the sauce is smooth and glossy.

Meanwhile, finely shred a quarter of the watercress leaves and set aside. In a clean pan, melt the remaining 30g butter. Add all the remaining watercress, season with salt, pepper and nutmeg and cook until the watercress is wilted. Remove from the heat and drain.

To serve, put the cooked watercress in the middle of four serving plates and surround each with three scallops. Add the shredded watercress to the sauce and pour around the scallops.

Created by Jonathan Batchelor, Ramus

COQUILLES PIERRE

Serves Four as a Starter	300g Gruyère cheese, grated
	Garlic butter *(see top tip below)*
48 Queen scallops *(4 per shell)*	Breadcrumbs *(made from 8 slices of white bread)*
12 Queen scallop shells *(3 per person)*	Salt and pepper

METHOD – Pre-heat the grill or oven to 180C. Place 4 Queen scallops in each shell and season with salt and pepper. Add a knob of garlic butter and cover with gruyère cheese. Sprinkle with breadcrumbs and grill till golden brown.

TOP TIP – Make your own garlic butter by mixing 250g soft salted butter with 2 cloves of finely chopped garlic and 1 dsp of chopped parsley. Roll into a log shape, wrap in clingfilm and chill until required.

FISH FACT

Queen scallops are a different species to King scallops and will never grow to the same size.

WINE MATCH – For red try a New World Pinot Noir or for white try a New World oaked Chardonnay.

16

Created by Jonathan Batchelor, Ramus
Shellfish Stock by Nick Rayner, Chef

___

LOBSTER THERMIDOR TARTLETS

___

<u>*Makes 16 tartlets*</u>

16 tartlet cases
Meat of ½ lobster
25g butter
2 large shallots finely chopped
150ml of fish stock

25ml brandy or white wine
50ml of double cream
½ tbsp of English mustard
1 tbsp parsley, chopped
Squeeze lemon juice
Salt and pepper
20g grated parmesan

___

METHOD – Pre-heat oven to 180°C.

For the tartlets: Add butter to a hot pan; add the shallots and sauté until soft. Add the stock, wine and double cream and bring to the boil. Reduce by half. While the mixture is reducing chop the lobster meat into small pieces and ¾ fill the tartlet cases.

When the mixture has reduced add the mustard, parsley and lemon juice and half the parmesan. Season to taste. Pour the mixture over the lobster meat in the cases and cook in the oven for 3 minutes. Sprinkle the remaining parmesan over and grill for 1 minute.

___

TOP TIP – Use the lobster shells to make a delicious shellfish stock.

___

<u>*Shellfish Stock*</u>
1 kg shellfish heads and shells
100g shallots & 2 celery sticks
2 carrots & 1 leek
3 garlic cloves & 1 red pepper

100g fennel & 50g tomato purée
Fresh herbs: ½ bunch thyme, 3 bay leaves, parsley stalk
2 star anise
250ml dry white wine
2 litres of water or fish stock for extra flavour

___

METHOD – Put everything into a saucepan and bring to the boil. Simmer for 1½ hours skimming off any scum every 15 minutes as this will make the stock cloudy and bitter. Sieve through muslin and then reduce down as required.

MOULES MARINIÈRE

Serves Two

1kg fresh Shetland rope grown mussels
1 large banana shallot
1 clove garlic, chopped

1 glass dry white wine
1 knob butter
400ml double cream
Salt and pepper
Parsley, small bunch, chopped

METHOD – Sauté the chopped shallot and garlic in a high sided pan until soft. Add the wine and bring to the boil. Add the mussels and steam for 2-3 minutes until open.

Remove the mussels and add the butter and the cream to the remaining liquor. Season with salt and pepper and remove from heat.

Place the mussels in a serving bowl and pour over the sauce. Garnish with the parsley and serve with chunks of crusty bread and a nice glass of chilled white wine.

FISH FACT

Not only are mussels the most environmentally sustainable shellfish, they also have the most impressive beneficial effects: Great for the heart, brain and reducing arthritis inflammation. Mussels even contain levels of iron and folic acid to rival red meat.

WINE MATCH – Muscadet or Picpoul de Pinet
(which is also perfect with oysters)

CAMOMILE TISANE MUSSELS WITH FENNEL AND WHITE WINE

Serves Two

3 dried tbsp of camomile tops – *Six tea bags will be enough for the recipe. Crush these in a pestle and mortar until they form a powder.*

1¼ kg mussels
1 large head of fennel, shredded
3 cloves of garlic, peeled & crushed
3 large shallots, peeled & chopped
200ml of medium/dry white wine
2 tablespoons of rapeseed oil

METHOD – Simply heat a high sided pan with the oil. Add the garlic, shallots and fennel and cook until softened with a lid on. This will take 1–2 minutes. Add the crushed heads of camomile and the washed mussels. Pour the white wine inside and put a tight fitting lid on the top.

Continue cooking the pan with a full heat until all the mussels open, shaking often. Remove them and place in a bowl for serving. Remember, everyone will enjoy some of that lovely camomile juice. Place a few delicate fennel swathes on top to garnish and serve with a bowl for the shells and finger bowls whilst eating the mussels.

TOP TIP – Remember to scrape off any barnacles from the mussels with a blunt knife and remove the beards – just a swift tug and they will come off. Always wash mussels before cooking.

Recipe & Image supplied by Fish is the Dish (a Seafish initiative)
www.fishisthedish.co.uk

CLAM LINGUINE

Serves Four

60 fresh clams
200g linguine
3 tbsp extra virgin olive oil, plus
extra for drizzling

1 tsp red chilli, finely sliced
1 tsp garlic, finely chopped
150ml Italian white wine
1 tbsp flat leaf parsley, chopped
Salt & fresh ground pepper
Lemon wedges, to serve

METHOD – Leave the clams to soak in cold water for 2 hours. Drain and rinse under cold running water, removing any sandy deposits from the shells. Discard any broken or damaged shells.

Cook the linguine in a large saucepan of salted water. Heat the oil in a saucepan over a medium heat. Add the chilli and garlic and gently fry for a minute until slightly coloured. Add the clams, cover the pan tightly and cook for 20 seconds, shaking the pan, until the clams open. Discard any that remain closed.

Pour in the white wine and simmer gently for 5 minutes. Remove from the heat. Using a perforated spoon, remove the clams from the pan. Remove the shells from half of them and return the clam flesh to the pan.

Drain the pasta and add to the clams. Stir in the parsley and season with salt & pepper. Toss to mix and drizzle with a few drops of olive oil.

Arrange the pasta equally on plates with the clam mixture. Serve immediately with a wedge of lemon.

FISH FACT

The speed at which the clam shuts its shell when threatened has lent its name to the idiom 'to clam up' meaning to keep your mouth shut and not say anything.

Recipe supplied by Fish is the Dish (a Seafish initiative)
www.fishisthedish.co.uk

DEEP FRIED PRAWNS WITH SOUR CREAM & SMOKED PAPRIKA

Serves Two

16 cooked prawns, shelled
A few mange tout
A few green beans
2 baby corn, split in two
1 baby pepper, split in two
6 thin slices of chorizo
1 quantity of batter mix *(see below)*
or packet of batter mix
1 baby gem lettuce, shredded

Sour cream
Chives, chopped
½ tsp smoked paprika
Lemon juice, a good squeeze

Tempura Batter
125g of flour
5g of dried yeast
250ml of milk *(tepid)*
Pinch of salt

METHOD – For the batter: Dissolve the yeast in a little of the tepid milk, add to the rest of the milk, then stir into the flour to form a smooth batter, allow to stand covered until starting to bubble.

For the tempura prawns: Dip the prawns and pieces of vegetable individually in the batter. Place each piece into hot fat, 2cm deep in a wok. Fry until golden, then drain on kitchen paper. Fry the chorizo until crispy.

For the sour cream: Mix together sour cream with the chopped chives, smoked paprika and a squeeze of lemon juice to taste. Serve with shredded baby gem lettuce.

Created by Steenbergs
www.steenbergs.co.uk

HARISSA PRAWNS WITH FRAGRANT LEMONGRASS RICE

Serves Two

400g raw peeled prawns
Steenbergs organic Harissa powder
2 tsp groundnut oil
100 ml fish stock

25g butter
Pinch Steenbergs Perfect Salt
100g long grain rice
100ml boiling water
1 tsp Steenbergs dried Lemongrass

METHOD – Place the prawns, harissa and oil in a bowl and leave to marinate.

Place the rice and lemongrass into a pan and pour over the boiling water Place on the lid and boil for 2 minutes then remove from the heat and leave for 10 minutes.

Heat a frying pan until it is smoking. Add the prawns and fry until coloured. Pour in the fish stock and reduce by half.

Add in the butter and whisk together. Check for seasoning.

Fork the rice through and serve with the prawns, drizzle with sauce and enjoy!

FISH FACT

All prawn types have 5 pairs of legs.

Created by Jonathan Batchelor, Ramus

SQUID & CHORIZO SERVED WITH LEMON, GARLIC AND OLIVE OIL

Serves Two

450g of small cleaned and prepared squid
200g of diced Chorizo sausage
Zest and juice of a large lemon

3 cloves garlic, finely chopped
75 ml olive oil
2 tablespoons of chopped parsley
Salt and black pepper
Wild rocket

METHOD – To prepare the squid remove the tentacles, then wash and dry them with kitchen towel. Cut the squid body into rings and wash them in cold running water, pat them dry and add them to the tentacles. Squeeze over the lemon juice and leave for 5 minutes after which drain off any excess liquid.

Heat oil in a pan and add the garlic and lemon zest, cooking slowly as the pan comes up to the heat. When it is hot add the chorizo and fry for 2 minutes. Bring the heat back up and add the squid, frying for 1 to 2 minutes. Add the parsley and season with salt and pepper.

Serve straight away from the pan onto a bed of wild rocket with lemon wedges to squeeze over.

WINE MATCH – Try a Rioja Crianza or a floral Riesling or Pinot Grigio

FISH RECIPES

28 - 67

─── FISH FACT ───

The French call bass 'loup de mer', wolf of the
sea, due to their voracious predatory nature.

HOW TO...
FILLET A SEA BASS

1. Scale fish from tail to head. Slice belly of fish from tail to head, cut around head leaving head intact then draw knife from head to tail on top of back bone.

2. Open out fillet and draw knife over and around ribcage to extract whole fillet.

3. Turn over and repeat.

4. Remove pin bones with tweezers.

This process can be used on all round fish.

HOW TO...
BUTTERFLY A MACKEREL

1. Slice belly from tail to head and remove guts.

2. Cut diagonally around fins on both sides, cutting off head.

3. Coming up from the belly, slice from top to bottom following the backbone, without going all the way through the fish. Repeat on both sides.

4. Remove bone with scissors leaving tail intact. Trim away darker belly/ribcage from side of fillet.

HOW TO...
BOAT FILLET A SEA BASS

1. Scale fish from tail to head. Trim all fins with scissors. Then slice on top of backbone from head to ¾ way down fish.

2. Turn over and repeat.

3. Expose both sides of the backbone.

4. Cut the backbone at both head and tail with scissors and remove. Remove guts. Empty cavity is now ready to stuff.

HOW TO...
FILLET A PLAICE

1. Start on white side. This is the thinner side so therefore slightly harder to fillet. Lay plaice flat and cut around head.

2. From back of head, place knife on top of backbone and slice carefully from head to tail.

3. Open exposed fillet and slice from tail to head with knife over central ridge of bone.

4. Slice fillet away from bone. Turn over and repeat process on other side.

This process can be used for all flat fish.

Recipe & Image supplied by Fish is the Dish (a Seafish initiative)
www.fishisthedish.co.uk

TERIYAKI STYLE FILLET OF GILT HEAD BREAM WITH NOODLES

Serves Four

4 fillets of Bream, pin-boned
200ml soy sauce
1 red chilli, chopped

8 good sprigs of coriander, chopped
2 glacé stem ginger, chopped or
equivalent fresh ginger, grated
2 tbsp honey
250g noodles

METHOD – Place soy sauce, chilli, coriander, ginger and honey into a liquidiser and liquidise.

Add to fish and leave overnight, or for at least 2 hours.

Remove fish from marinade. Pan fry fish skin side down in a little olive oil, for 2-3 minutes then turn to cook on other side.

Cook noodles in boiling water then drain and toss in a little of the fish marinade. Serve fish on top of noodles with extra sauce drizzled over as required.

Recipe & Image supplied by Fish is the Dish (a Seafish initiative)
www.fishisthedish.co.uk

FISH STEW

Serves Four

550g skinned and cubed whitefish
fillets *(cod, coley, pollack, hake)*
115g mussels
15ml sunflower oil
225g carrots
1 onion

1 clove garlic
1 x 397g can peeled
chopped tomatoes
6 black olives
1 bay leaf
Salt and black pepper
Chopped parsley to garnish

METHOD – Peel the carrots and cut them into sticks. Slice the onion and crush the garlic.

Heat the oil in a saucepan and add all these ingredients, then cook for 2-3 minutes. Stir in the tomatoes, olives and bay leaf, and season to taste.

Add the fish and cook for another 8-10 minutes. The mussels go in last and need about 2-4 minutes to heat through as they open up.

Sprinkle on the chopped parsley and serve with lots of crusty bread.

FISH FACT

Pollock is only spelt with an 'o' at the end when it comes from Alaska and is a different (albeit similar) species to our Atlantic Pollack.

Created by Jonathan Batchelor, Ramus
Fish Stock by Nick Rayner, Chef

PAN FRIED LOIN OF COD WITH PEA PURÉE

Serves Two

2 x 200g loins of cod
200g frozen garden peas
2 sprigs fresh mint, leaves chopped

1 tsp mint sauce
200ml fish or vegetable stock
Knob of butter
Olive oil
Salt and pepper & flour

METHOD – To make the pea purée, cook the garden peas in the stock and then either crush or preferably purée them in a food blender. Add a glug of olive oil, a spoonful of mint sauce and then some chopped fresh mint. Season to taste.

Preheat the oven to 180˚C. Season the flour with salt and pepper and roll the cod in the seasoned flour. Add a glug of oil and a knob of butter to a hot pan and then add the cod skin side down, pan frying for 2 to 3 mins until skin is crisp. Transfer to a hot oven (180˚C) for 8-10 minutes until cod cooked through.

Serve on the pea purée with fried new potatoes.

TOP TIP – For an extra creamy pea purée, blend in 1 tablespoon of crème fraîche.

Fish Stock
2.5 kg fish bones and trim
*(freely available at Ramus on request, best ones
being flatfish such as lemon sole or plaice)*
1 onion, chopped

1 celery stick, chopped
½ small bulb of fennel *(including leaves)*, chopped
1 bay leaf
1 leek, just white part, chopped
2 glasses of dry white wine

METHOD – Soften chopped vegetables in a little olive oil or butter. Add bones and wine and top up with water to cover. Bring to boil and then simmer for 20 minutes (no longer otherwise stock will become bitter), skimming off any scum that appears.

Created by Amy Callin, Senior Tutor, Bettys Cookery School
www.bettyscookeryschool.co.uk

FISH PIE

Serves Four

For the topping
3 large potatoes
1 sweet potato
30ml double cream

For the filling
50ml white wine
500ml fish stock
(made up with 1 stock cube)
1 onion, finely chopped
1 leek, cut in half and chopped
2 bay leaves
300g haddock fillet, skinned

and cut into 2cm cubes
200g salmon fillet, skinned
and cut into 2 cm cubes
150g raw tiger prawns,
shelled and deveined
Salt and ground black pepper

For the sauce
50g butter
50g plain flour
350ml fish liquor *(see method)*
150ml double or whipping cream
2 tsp Dijon mustard
2 tbsp chopped parsley
Salt and ground black pepper

METHOD – Place the white potato in a pan of cold salted water. Bring to the boil and then add the sweet potato. Simmer for 10-15 minutes or until the potatoes are soft, but not broken up. Remove from the heat, drain and return to the pan so they can dry out for a few minutes before mashing. Stir in the double cream and lightly season.

In a large saucepan, bring the wine to the boil and add the stock. Add the onion, leek and bay leaf and simmer for few minutes to allow the onion and leek to braise. Add the fish and prawns and simmer for a further 2-3 minutes or until the fish is just cooked. Strain the poaching liquor into a measuring jug and place the fish and vegetables back in the pan. In a separate saucepan, make the sauce by melting the butter, adding the flour to the butter and mixing continuously. Add the flour to the butter, mixing continuously until

it becomes a smooth paste and begins to bubble.
Remove from the heat and gradually whisk in the poaching liquor until it is all incorporated. Return to the heat and bring to the boil, stirring continuously until the sauce is thick and smooth. Pour in the double cream, stir in the Dijon mustard, chopped parsley and season to taste.

To assemble and to cook the dish: Gently mix the sauce with the fish and then transfer to an ovenproof dish allowing enough room to top with the mashed potato. Spoon or pipe the mashed potato over the pie, ensuring it is fully covered to prevent the filling from leaking.

Place into a preheated oven for 20-25 minutes until piping hot and the mashed potato has started to colour.

Created by Chris Blackburn, Chef
www.yorkshirepudd.co.uk

YORKSHIRE FISH AND CHIPS WITH TARTARE SAUCE

Serves Two

Ingredients for the Fish and Chips
2 pieces of haddock
Seasoned flour
(1 tbsp plain flour mixed with 1 tsp sea salt & 1tsp cracked black pepper)
1 egg, beaten
400g Maris Piper potatoes peeled
Olive oil for frying

Ingredients for mayonnaise
2 free-range egg yolks
1 tsp English mustard
285ml / ½ pint groundnut oil
Pinch of sea salt and white pepper

Ingredients for tartare sauce
200ml of your
homemade mayonnaise
3 tbsp capers, drained
and finely chopped
3 tbsp cocktail gherkins,
drained and finely chopped
1 small shallot, finely chopped
Squeeze of lemon juice
3 tbsp chopped fresh parsley
Sea salt and freshly
ground black pepper

METHOD — First make the mayonnaise by placing the egg yolks into a mixing bowl; add the mustard, salt and pepper and mix all of them together well. Gradually begin to add the oil, a trickle at a time. Try using a mixer with the whisk attachment whilst drizzling in the oil. Ensure each drop of oil is thoroughly whisked before adding the next drop. When all the oil has been added, taste and add more salt and pepper if it needs it. Mix together all of the tartare sauce ingredients and combine well with 200ml of the mayonnaise. Preheat the oven to 200°C.

Chop the potatoes into ½ cm wedges, then coat or spray with light olive oil and bake for 20 minutes. In the meantime cut each piece of haddock lengthways and then across to give you 4 pieces of fish per fillet. Coat firstly in seasoned flour, then in beaten egg and finally in Panko breadcrumbs. Shallow fry the coated fish for 3-4 mins each side or until golden. Serve with the chips and a large dollop of tartare sauce.

MEDITERRANEAN HADDOCK WITH A TOMATO AND SMOKED PAPRIKA STEW

Serves Three

1 large haddock fillet
(bones removed)
1 red onion
1 white onion
1 fresh red chilli
1 orange pepper
1 tsp Steenbergs chilli powder
1 tsp Steenbergs garlic granules

1 tsp Steenbergs smoked paprika
3 tsp Steenbergs Mediterranean rub
1 pinch of Steenbergs lemon sugar
1 tin organic chopped tomatoes
1 handful of frozen peas
6 large white potatoes
30g butter
Salt and pepper
Steenbergs Fleur de Sel
1 spring onion to garnish

METHOD – For the sauce: Dice the red onion, white onion, orange pepper and chilli. Sweat together in a hot pan for a few minutes. Add in all the Steenbergs spices, herbs and flavoured sugar. Cook for 1 minute. Pour in the chopped tomatoes and season with salt and pepper. Bring to a simmer and allow to reduce until rich and thickened. Stir in the frozen peas at the last minute just to warm through.

For the mash: While the sauce is reducing, peel the potatoes, cut into quarters and bring to the boil in a pan of salted water. When cooked, drain and return to the dry pan, add salt, pepper and the butter and mash until smooth.

For the fish: Place a frying pan on the heat. Cut the fish fillet into portions, oil lightly and season with salt and pepper. Fry the fish skin down for 2 minutes, turn and finish cooking for a further minute or so.

TOP TIP – Add a little butter to the pan toward the end of the cooking time to get a lovely golden colour on the fish.

Spoon out the sauce into a large bowl, place the mash in the middle of the bowl and sit the fish fillet on the mash. Garnish with a little chopped chilli, spring onion and a few flakes of Steenbergs Fleur de Sel.

Created by Sue Nelson, Yorkshire Food Finder
www.yorkshirefoodfinder.org

YORKSHIRE BLUE SMOKED HADDOCK MORNAY

Serves Two

300g natural dye smoked
haddock loin, skinned
200g baby spinach leaves
250ml whipping cream
100ml fish stock
1 tsp wholegrain mustard
A glut of dry sherry

Small leek, white part only
50g breadcrumbs
(2 slices of white bread)
75g Yorkshire Blue cheese
Generous handful of chopped
parsley, dill and chives, mixed
Knob of butter
Freshly grated nutmeg
Seasoning

METHOD – Preheat the oven to 200°C. Wilt the spinach, drain and cool. Finely chop the leek and sauté in a little butter. Set aside.

In a sauté pan reduce the cream, fish stock and sherry by half until it begins to thicken. Add the wholegrain mustard and the cooked leeks.
Check the haddock for pin bones and dice into 2-3cm cubes. Whiz the bread in a food processor to make the breadcrumbs. Finely chop the herbs and add to the breadcrumbs. Set aside. Crumble the Yorkshire Blue cheese and set aside.

Using your hands, squeeze all the liquid out of the spinach. Grate nutmeg over and put a layer of the spinach in the bottom of two individual oven-proof shallow dishes.

Add the haddock and leek to the cream mixture and cook gently for 3-4 minutes until the fish begins to go opaque. Check the seasoning, adding more salt and pepper if required (note the fish is likely to be salty already from the smoking process, so go easy). Spoon the fish mixture into the dishes on top of the spinach layer.

Add the breadcrumbs and herb mix to cover and dot with the blue cheese. Bake in the hot oven for 10 minutes until the cheese has melted and the breadcrumbs are crisp and golden.

Created by Ivano de Serio, The Old Bakery Restaurant, Lincoln
Courtesy of Grimsby Traditional Smoked Fish Group

SMOKED HADDOCK AND FRESH HERB PÂTÉ WITH PARMESAN MAYONNAISE

Serves 20

Pâté
4 large smoked haddock fillets
½ clove of garlic, finely chopped
2 shallots, finely chopped
1 red, 1 yellow & 1 green pepper, finely diced
1 tbsp tarragon, freshly chopped
1 tbsp coriander, freshly chopped
1 tbsp dill, freshly chopped
1 tbsp chive, freshly chopped

200gr soft unsalted butter
(room temperature)
Pinch of ground nutmeg
900ml double cream
Black pepper and sea salt to taste

Mayonnaise
13 egg yolks
1 tsp Dijon mustard
2 tbsp warm white wine vinegar
200g grated parmesan cheese
500ml sunflower oil & salt

METHOD − In a deep pan sweat the shallots, the diced peppers and garlic, cook for 5 minutes and chill.

Place the double cream plus 1 litre of water in a deep pan and bring to boil. With the help of tweezers or fish boner, pick all the bones from the haddock and poach it in the cream for 15 minutes or until cooked. When ready, discard the skin and cool the haddock.

Place the cooked peppers, herbs, fish and butter in a bowl and gently mix making sure not to over mix to keep some chunks of haddock. Season with salt, pepper and ground nutmeg.

To make the mayonnaise, mix the egg yolks, mustard, vinegar and parmesan cheese in a blender, then blend in the oil gently a little at the time. Adjust the consistency with a little hot water if too thick.

Serve the pâté with a little bit of the mayo in a spoon or on a little toasted slice of bread.

TOP TIP − Reserve the cooking cream to make a delicious seafood soup or chowder.

SMOKED HADDOCK CHOWDER

<u>*Serves Four*</u>

500g smoked haddock
1 leek, diced *(reserving outer leaf)*
4 sticks celery, diced
1 white onion, diced
1 clove of garlic, finely chopped
2 potatoes, King Edward or
similar, peeled & medium diced
50g butter
1 glass dry white wine
1.5 litres vegetable stock

<u>*Bouquet garni*</u>
2 sprigs of rosemary, 2 sprigs
thyme, 2 bay leaves & 2
sprigs of tarragon wrapped
up in outer leaf of leek like a
parcel and tied with string.
250ml double cream
200g sweetcorn, tinned or frozen
200g peas, frozen

METHOD – Sweat the garlic, leek, celery, onion, potato & bouquet garni in a large knob of butter until soft but not coloured.

Add dry white wine and vegetable stock and season well with salt and pepper. Bring to the boil and then simmer until vegetables are cooked and soft.

Just before serving remove bouquet garni, then add double cream, smoked haddock, sweetcorn and peas, simmering for 5 minutes until fish is cooked. Serve immediately with fresh crusty bread.

TOP TIP – For a seafood chowder, add a handful of mussels at the last minute, put the lid on and cook for 2 minutes until shells open up. Discard any that do not open.

FILLET OF HAKE WITH MILD CURRY POTATO, LIME & CUCUMBER DRESSING & PRAWN BHAJI

Serves Four

The Hake
4 x 6-8oz hake portions with skin
1dsp garam masala
60g butter
Salt & Pepper
1 lemon

Mild Curry Potato
16 new potatoes, cooked and roughly chopped
60g butter
1 small onion, finely diced
1 dsp mild curry powder
½ clove of garlic, crushed

Cucumber dressing
½ cucumber peeled, and diced
a few springs of mint chopped
1 lime & 4 tbsp natural yoghurt

Prawn Bhaji
1dsp vegetable oil
1 onion thinly sliced
1 egg beaten & plain flour
1 small bunch of coriander, chopped
200g prawns, well drained
½ clove of garlic, crushed
pinch of ground cumin, chilli powder & turmeric
Vegetable oil for deep frying

METHOD – Place the hake portions skin side down on a plate, sprinkle the flesh with salt, pepper and the garam masala and leave in the fridge for 2 hours.

For the dressing: Juice and zest the lime into a bowl, add the yoghurt, cucumber and mint and season with salt and pepper. Refrigerate until required.

For the bhaji: In a saucepan warm the vegetable oil, add the sliced onion and garlic and cook slowly to soften. Once the onion is soft add the spices and cook for another minute. Put the contents of the pan into a bowl and cool slightly. Add the prawns, coriander and egg and stir together. Add plain flour a bit at a time until the ingredients start to hold together. This is best done in advance so you can drop spoonfuls of the batter into the fryer to cook.

Pre heat the oven to 200°C, pre heat the fryer. Heat a heavy bottomed non-stick ovenproof frying pan with a dash of vegetable oil and a sprinkle of salt. Place the hake skin side down in the pan and put a knob of butter on each hake portion. Cook in the oven for 5 minutes. Meanwhile melt 60g of butter in a saucepan, add the diced onion, garlic and curry powder and cook for a minute. Add the chopped new potatoes and break them up with a fork and keep them moving to heat them up. Take the hake out of the oven and squeeze the juice of the lemon over the hake. Turn each portion over and return to the oven for a couple more minutes to finish cooking. Carefully place dollops of the bhaji mix into the fryer and cook, once cooked drain well on kitchen paper. When the hake is cooked and the potatoes are warm assemble the dish and finish with the yoghurt dressing.

CRAB CRUSTED FILLET OF HAKE WITH SEASONAL GREENS AND SHELLFISH MAYONNAISE

Serves Four

4 hake portions
(approx. 200g each)

For the crab crust
1 crab, dressed
100g Japanese (panko) breadcrumbs
3 medium tomatoes
2 medium shallots
1 chilli
Parsley, good sprinkle
1 lemon
50ml extra virgin olive oil
Sea salt, good pinch

Shellfish mayonnaise
3 egg yolks
50ml white wine vinegar
1 dsp Dijon mustard
100ml shellfish sauce
(instructions below)
300ml vegetable oil

Shellfish sauce
500g langoustine shells
2 medium carrots
1 medium onion
3 cloves of garlic
2 celery sticks
125ml white wine
50ml brandy
2 star anise
1 tsp peppercorns
2 bay leaves

METHOD – Preheat oven to 180°C. First make the shellfish sauce: Place your langoustine shells in the pre-heated oven and roast for 15 minutes until the shells are all a pale colour. While this is cooking, peel vegetables and roughly chop, heat a pan with a splash of oil and sweat vegetables without colouring. Add white wine and brandy and reduce by half. After 10 minutes add your shells and all the juices to the vegetables followed by the star anise, peppercorns and the bay leaves. Next add cold water to just cover the shells, bring to boil and turn down the heat to a simmer for 30 minutes. After this, strain the stock and discard the shells. Put your stock back on the heat and reduce down until the stock starts to thicken slightly and turns a darker colour. Season with salt & pepper to taste and chill until required.

For the mayonnaise: In a food processor add your egg yolks, white wine vinegar, Dijon mustard and shell fish sauce (above). Blend for 1 minute until the mixture becomes pale in colour. Then slowly add the vegetable oil until it emulsifies. This will make a thick mayonnaise, to thin out add lemon juice and season to taste.

Next the crab crust: Chop tomatoes into quarters and remove the fleshy middle and seeds then dice into small chunks. Peel shallots and dice. Roughly chop parsley, add the breadcrumbs, olive oil, chili and lemon then mix all ingredients in a bowl. Remove meat from crab and add to bowl and gently hand mix combining ingredients together.

Place hake in oven skin side up for 10 minutes. After 10 minutes place the crab crust on top of the skin and cook for a further 6 minutes. Whilst the hake is cooking, prep your seasonal greens, in this case we are using tender stem broccoli, blanch until cooked in boiling water.

To serve, place the vegetables in the center of plate with hake resting on top, and finish with a drizzle of shellfish mayo. Bon appetite!

Created by Mitch Tonks, Restaurateur & Food Writer
Taken from FISH *by Mitch Tonks published by Pavilion, Image by Chris Terry*

GRILLED JOHN DORY WITH BRAISED FENNEL AND ANCHOVY VINAIGRETTE

Serves Four

150 ml olive oil
150 ml white wine vinegar
150 ml white wine
2 bay leaves
1 tsp fennel seeds
1 tsp coriander seeds
1 sliced lemon
1 small onion, finely sliced
3 cloves garlic, finely sliced
3 Florence fennel bulbs

4 x John Dory fillets
(they will vary in size but allow about 180g per person)
Salt

For the anchovy vinaigrette
6 salted anchovy fillets
1 tsp Dijon mustard
3 tbsp white wine vinegar
100 ml double cream
1 tbsp parsley, finely chopped
Squeeze of lemon
Black pepper

METHOD – Pre heat the oven to 175°C. First braise the fennel by gently heating the olive oil, wine vinegar, wine, bay leaf, fennel seeds and coriander seeds in a pan. Then add the sliced lemon, onion, sliced garlic and fennel. Cover and cook in the oven for about an hour until the fennel is tender. Remove from the oven and allow to cool at room temperature in the braising liquid.

Make the anchovy vinaigrette by pounding the anchovy fillets in a pestle and mortar. Then put the mustard in a bowl with the vinegar and whisk together slowly adding the olive oil until those 3 ingredients emulsify. Then add the anchovy paste and gently whisk in the cream. Add the parsley, a squeeze of lemon and plenty of black pepper.

Heat the grill then brush the John Dory fillets with a little olive oil and season with salt. Grill for 6-7 minutes until lightly golden.

To serve put 2 or 3 chunks of braised fennel and onion mixture on a plate, place the fish alongside and drizzle with the anchovy vinaigrette.

MONKFISH WITH FRIED POTATOES & PARMA HAM

Serves Two

2 good sized portions of
monkfish tail, trimmed
2 potatoes, sliced lengthways
2 ready marinated artichoke hearts
4-6 slices Parma ham

1 dsp capers
1 dsp flat leaf
parsley, chopped
¼ lemon, squeezed
½ glass dry white wine
Olive oil
Salt & pepper

METHOD – Peel potatoes & par-boil keeping firm, then slice lengthways
into 1cm slices.

Sauté potatoes in hot pan with a little olive oil until golden, add artichokes
and pan fry for 2 minutes until nicely coloured.

In a separate pan, heat a glug of oil and a knob of butter. Sear and colour the
fish before finishing off in a pre heated oven (180˚C) for 7 minutes.

Once the fish is cooked, remove from the pan but keep warm. Deglaze the
pan with the white wine, add the capers and parsley and a squeeze of lemon.

Assemble the dish by placing the potatoes on a plate and layering with the
artichokes, Parma ham and then the fish. Finish off by spooning over the pan
juices.

Created by Jonathan Batchelor, Ramus
—

SPICY MONKFISH WITH MINT YOGHURT

Serves Two

400g monkfish, trimmed
(200g per person, making 2 kebabs each)

Spicy glaze
1 tsp harissa paste & 1 tsp dry spice blend, mixed
with a little olive oil.
(Steenbergs organic Tagine blend works very well)
Alternatively use any ready made tandoori paste.

Mint yoghurt
250ml natural yoghurt
1 tsp mint sauce & zest ½ lemon
¼ deseeded cucumber, finely chopped
1 tsp caster sugar

Iceberg lettuce
Salt & pepper

METHOD – Season the monkish with salt and pepper and then marinate in the spicy glaze for 30 minutes. Cut the fish into chunks and assemble the kebabs.

Mix all of the ingredients for the mint yoghurt in a bowl and refrigerate until needed.

Pan-fry or barbecue the monkfish kebabs for 2 to 3 minutes on each side and serve on a bed of shredded iceberg lettuce with lemon wedges and some of the mint yoghurt.

TOP TIP – If cooking on the barbecue, make sure to soak the kebab sticks in water to avoid burning.

WINE MATCH – Try a fruity Australian Shiraz,
New World Pinot Noir or Riesling

Created by Mohammed Aslam, Aagrah Group of Restaurants
www.aagrah.com

MUMBAI MACHLI

Serves Four

500g monkfish, cut into cubes
Vegetable oil for deep frying
6 dsp olive oil
1 medium onion, chopped
6 cloves of garlic, crushed or grated
1 dsp ginger purée
3 medium tomatoes, chopped
2 dsp natural yoghurt
½ dsp red chilli powder
¼ dsp turmeric powder
½ dsp salt
1 dsp coriander seeds, ground

½ dsp cumin seeds, ground
6 bay leaves
½ dsp garam masala
4 fresh red chillies, whole
1 handful of fresh coriander
6 fresh curry leaves
½ fresh lime, sliced

Ingredients for Marinade
½ dsp garlic purée
¼ dsp ajwain seeds, ground
1 dsp natural yoghurt
¼ dsp salt

METHOD – Marinate the monkfish with the ingredients in the marinade
(the longer you leave it, the more intense the flavours). Then heat vegetable
oil in a deep sided pan and deep fry the marinated fish until half cooked.

Heat olive oil in pan and fry onion until light brown. Add garlic, ginger and
tomatoes and fry together with onion (for extra gravy add more onion).

Add yoghurt and fry for a few minutes, then add red chilli powder,
turmeric powder and salt, followed by ground coriander, ground cumin
and bay leaves.

Add in the fish, garam masala, red chillies, fresh coriander and fresh curry
leaves and cook gently. Finally add the lime and cook for a few minutes.

Serve with freshly steamed basmati rice.

RED MULLET WITH PEA RISOTTO & TAPENADE DRESSING

Serves Six

Tapenade Dressing
100g pitted olives
1 clove garlic, finely chopped
1 tsp fresh thyme leaves *(no stalks)*
1 anchovy fillet, very
finely chopped
150ml olive oil

Pea Purée
300g frozen peas
200ml chicken stock
50g unsalted butter

Risotto
½ onion finely chopped
1 clove garlic, finely chopped
50g unsalted butter
150g arborio rice
300-400ml chicken stock *(warmed)*
50g freshly grated parmesan
12 tablespoons of the Pea Purée
Salt & pepper

Red Mullet
12 red mullet fillets
(2 per person if small)
pin-boned and scaled
2 cloves garlic, peeled & sliced
Squeeze lemon juice
Chopped sun dried tomatoes
& frisee lettuce for garnish

METHOD — To make the tapenade, put the olives, thyme, garlic and anchovy into a blender, turn on and slowly drizzle in the oil until all combined. Store chilled until needed.

To make the pea purée, place peas, stock and pinch of salt in a pan, cook until tender. Put in a liquidiser, add the butter, and purée until smooth. Season to taste & set aside until needed.

To make the risotto, melt the butter in a wide based non stick pan & gently cook the onion and garlic without colouring (about 2 mins).
Add the rice & stir well, coating the rice with butter, onion and garlic mix.

Add the stock, a little at a time, stirring continuously so the rice does not stick and cooks evenly. When the stock has been absorbed, add a little more, continue until rice is almost cooked (it is cooked when firm, but must not be crunchy). Now add the parmesan and pea purée, mix well, season and keep warm.

Next, drizzle some oil over the fish. Heat a large non stick pan and place some grease proof paper in the bottom (this will help the skin from sticking, even in a non stick pan). Place the fish in, skin side down, and cook for 2-3 mins until skin is crisp. Flip over, place some garlic on top, a squeeze of lemon and remove from heat. Allow to sit for 1-2 mins and serve.

Created by Jonathan Batchelor, Ramus

PAN FRIED GIGHA HALIBUT WITH SALSA VERDE

Serves Eight

8 x 140g fillets of Gigha Halibut, skinned
Plain flour *(seasoned with sea salt & black pepper)*
Olive oil & butter for pan-frying

1½–2 cloves of garlic, peeled
1 small handful of capers
1 small handful of gherkins pickled in sweet vinegar

6 anchovy fillets
2 large handfuls of flat-leaf parsley, leaves picked
1 bunch of fresh basil, leaves picked
1 handful of fresh mint, leaves picked
1 tbsp Dijon mustard
3 tbsps red wine vinegar
8 tbsps really good extra virgin olive oil
sea salt and freshly ground black pepper

METHOD – _Salsa Verde_ – Finely chop all the ingredients together adding the oil at the end to ensure the correct consistency. Season the salsa with salt and black pepper to taste. This can now be refrigerated until you are ready to cook the fish.

Dust the halibut in flour seasoned with a salt and pepper. Add oil and a knob of butter to a hot pan and cook for 2 to 3 minutes on both sides depending upon the thickness. Serve on top of the Salsa Verde.

WINE MATCH – New World Pinot Noir,
New World Merlot or Chablis

GRILLED HALIBUT FILLET, SMOKED SALMON, BROWN SHRIMPS & BROAD BEANS

Serves Four

4 pieces of halibut, skinned
Salt and pepper
Smoked paprika
150g fresh or frozen broad beans
White wine, small glass

2 shallots, finely chopped
2 tbsp white wine vinegar
150g smoked salmon
4 tbsp double cream
200g unsalted butter
100g brown shrimps
Olive oil

METHOD — Wash and dry the halibut well & place in a small flat dish, add a drizzle of olive oil, salt and pepper and a pinch of smoked paprika. Coat the fish well with the oil and seasoning & leave in the fridge covered until needed.

Preheat your griddle pan on a low gas and pod the broad beans if necessary. In a medium saucepan place the glass of white wine, shallots, white wine vinegar and finely chopped smoked salmon. Bring to the boil and simmer for 2 minutes. Add the broad beans, cream and brown shrimps and cook for a further 2 minutes.

Cut the butter into small cubes, add to the hot mixture and stir constantly until the butter has melted totally. Get the non stick griddle pan very hot and place the 4 pieces of halibut gently in the pan.

Reduce the heat a little once the fish is seared. Leave to cook for 3 minutes then turn over & cook for a further 3 minutes before turning off the heat.

Leave the fish in the pan for another 4 minutes as it will slowly carry on cooking. Serve immediately with the sauce over the fish.

TOP TIP — Double pod the broad beans to reveal the nutty bean inside, by removing the thick outer skin with your finger.

FILLET OF PLAICE WITH MUSSELS, SAMPHIRE AND SALSIFY IN A BURNT CREAM SAUCE AND JERUSALEM ARTICHOKE PURÉE

Serves Four

8 fillets of plaice
500g mussels
½ onion, diced
1 small carrot, diced
1 small fennel, diced
4 cloves garlic, crushed
2 bay leaves
4 sprigs of lemon thyme or thyme
250ml white wine

100ml water
500g whipping cream
Juice ½ lemon
200g Jerusalem artichokes
40g smoked Yorkshire rapeseed oil
50g butter
½ lemon
300g salsify
50g samphire
30g sea purslane *(optional)*
5g tarragon leaves

METHOD – Remove the fillets from the plaice and set aside (see p33), wash and chop the bones, set aside or freeze to make fish stock with at a later date (see p37).

Rinse the mussels under cold water for 10 minutes to remove any grit. Pull the beards off the mussels. Combine with the chopped vegetables, garlic and herbs.

In a suitable large pan bring the wine to the boil, add the water and return to boil. Add the mussels and veg mix and cover. Cook until the mussels open, around 3 minutes on high heat.

Strain the liquid off and reserve. Give the pan a quick rinse and add the mussel stock to the pan, reduce the liquid down till almost nothing remains. While this is happening pick the mussels out of the shells, this is easiest when they are still warm, store in the fridge till needed later.

Once the stock is reduced add a third of the cream & keeping on a high heat, stir the cream until it starts to catch and burn. Add another third of the cream, repeat again until all the cream is used, you want the sauce to be thick. Strain through a sieve, reserve till later. Peel the salsify into water with some lemon juice in to prevent browning, chop to ½ cm pieces and simmer in seasoned water till just tender. Set aside till later.

Chop the Jerusalem artichokes and simmer in water with the lemon until tender. Drain and purée adding only a little water (plus seasoning) to create a thick purée. Pick any woody stalks off the samphire and pick the leaves off the sea purslane.

To serve: Heat all the vegetables and mussels in the burnt cream, adding the tarragon at the last minute. Heat a little oil in a non stick pan, season the plaice with salt and pepper and fry for 2-3 miutes each side until golden brown. Add a quenelle of purée on the side.

KIPPER KEDGEREE

2 smoked Swallow Fish kippers
450ml boiling water
25g butter
1 onion, finely chopped
1 tsp hot curry powder
225g basmati rice
110ml double cream

Lemon, juice only
Salt & black pepper
3 eggs, hard-boiled, peeled,
roughly chopped
3 tbsp roughly chopped
fresh flat leaf parsley

METHOD – Place the kippers into a deep baking dish and pour over the boiling water. Leave in the water for five minutes, then remove and set aside, reserving the soaking liquid. Carefully remove the meat from the fish, taking care to remove all the bones. Place the kipper meat into a bowl and set aside.

Meanwhile, heat a deep frying pan with a lid until hot then add the butter. Once the butter has melted, add the onion and fry for 3-4 minutes, until just softened but not coloured.

Add the curry powder and cook for a further minute, then add the rice and stir to coat well in the butter and onions. Add the reserved kipper soaking liquid and heat to a gentle simmer, then cover with the lid and cook for 12-15 minutes, until the rice is tender and all the liquid has been absorbed. Stir in the double cream and lemon juice.

Season to taste with salt and freshly ground black pepper, then add the kipper meat, eggs and parsley. Stir gently to combine without breaking up the kipper meat too much. To serve, spoon into warmed bowls.

SPICED WHITBY MACKEREL FILLET WITH MANGO AND CORIANDER SALAD

Serves Two

1 large mackerel, filleted
and pin bones removed
2 large bamboo skewers, pre-soaked
½ tsp finely chopped green chilli
3 limes
Pinch of fennel pollen
8 leaves of baby gem salad
1 small bunch of coriander

1 mango
1 carrot
1 small bunch of samphire
1 cucumber
1 large shallot
1 tsp honey
3 tbsp rapeseed oil
1 tbsp Lemon, Basil,
Bay & Juniper Vinegar
from Womersley Vinegars

METHOD – For the fish: Gently sprinkle the mackerel with fennel pollen or cracked black pepper if you prefer. Cut a lime in half and then again into three segments before placing the lime and the mackerel on the bamboo skewer that has been pre-soaked in water. Rub the chilli, fennel pollen and a little zest and juice of lime over the mackerel and allow to marinade. This can be done overnight for a strong marinade or used straightaway if you prefer. Make sure the barbecue is hot or use a hot chargrill pan. Cook the mackerel for around two minutes each side depending on the size of the fish.

For the salad: Peel and destone the mango before cutting it into thin pieces. Add half the coriander leaves, the grated carrot and the baby gem lettuce. Blanch the samphire by quickly dropping it into boiling water before refreshing under a cold tap and adding half to the salad. Peel four strands of cucumber vertically down the whole cucumber.

For the dressing: Finely chop the shallot and the remaining coriander leaves and samphire. Add to this the zest and juice of the limes, a teaspoon of honey and one tablespoon of the Womersley Vinegar. Whisk this together and pour the rapeseed oil slowly into the bowl whisking all the time.

Pour the dressing over the salad leaves. You may not use all the dressing so keep it for your next salad. Place the hot skewer of mackerel onto the salad and serve with some of the dressing around the plate.

BEETROOT CURED SALMON

<u>*Serves 8-10*</u>

<u>*Cure*</u>
Side of salmon *(approx. 2kg)*
4 large beetroot
2 lemons *(zest and juice)*
150g sea salt
2 shots of Smirnoff vodka

<u>*Topping*</u>
Bunch of fresh dill *(50-75g)*
150g wholegrain mustard
2 lemons *(zest and juice)*

METHOD – Lay the salmon fillet, skin side down, on a board and brush your hand along it. If you feel any little pin bones, pinch them out with your fingers or tweezers.

In a food processor, mix all of the ingredients for the salmon together to make the cure.

Stretch two large sheets of cling film over a work surface and spoon over the cure, then place the salmon on top and wrap tightly with lots of cling film. Place in a container, such as a large roasting tray, then put a smaller tray on top over the salmon and weigh it down (with a couple of tins, for example). Leave in the fridge for at least three days or up to a week. Don't be alarmed by the amount of liquid that leaks out, this is normal.

To serve, unwrap the salmon from the cling film and brush off the marinade. Mix all the topping ingredients together and put on top of the salmon. Once made, the salmon will sit happily in the fridge for up to a week.

Serve by cutting it into thin slices as you would with smoked salmon.

Created by Wester Ross Fisheries, Scotland
Image by Polished

HERBY STEAMED SALMON

Serves Four

4 x 175g Wester Ross salmon fillets
150ml water
1 bunch of coriander, washed
and roughly chopped
18 mint leaves
3 crushed garlic cloves

½ tsp salt
3 green chillies, no seeds
Juice and zest of 2 limes
1 tbsp runny honey
2 tsp fresh ginger, peeled and grated
1 tbsp fish sauce
Stir-fried noodles and
vegetables, to serve

METHOD – For the dressing, place the coriander leaves and stalks, mint leaves, garlic, salt and chillies into a food processor and whizz into a paste. Add the lime juice and zest, honey, ginger and fish sauce and process.

Place the salmon in a bowl and spoon over half the dressing. Marinate for 20-30 minutes.

Bring the water to the boil in the bottom half of the steamer. Wipe most of the marinade off the salmon. Place the bowl with the marinated salmon in the top half and steam for 4-6 minutes. Remove from the steamer and leave to sit for a minute.

Serve the salmon on a bed of stir-fried noodles and vegetables drizzled with the remaining dressing.

SMOKED SALMON FLORENTINE

Serves Two

2 breakfast muffins, halved
& lightly toasted
2 large handfuls of spinach
Knob of butter
Salt & pepper
4 slices of smoked salmon
4 eggs

Hollandaise Sauce
6 egg yolks
500g butter, clarified if possible
75ml white wine vinegar
(alternatively 50ml lemon juice)
6 black peppercorns

METHOD – First make the hollandaise sauce by hand whisking the egg yolks in a bowl over a pan of simmering water until thick and light in colour.

Simmer the white wine vinegar with the peppercorns in a separate pan until reduced by two-thirds. Strain out the peppercorns and add the vinegar reduction to the whisked eggs. Finally slowly incorporate the hot clarified butter, whisking all the time until you have a smooth emulsion.

Next wilt the spinach in a pan with a knob of butter and season with salt and pepper. Poach the eggs in a pan of simmering water with a dash of white wine vinegar for 2½ minutes.

Assemble the Florentine by placing a spoonful of spinach on each muffin, followed by a slice of smoked salmon and then a poached egg. Finally spoon the hollandaise sauce on top and season with freshly ground black pepper and a sprinkling of sea salt.

TOP TIP – If your hollandaise splits, just add a little hot water and mix well.

RAINBOW TROUT WITH LEMONY CAPER BUTTER

Serves Four

4 rainbow trout, filleted *(8 fillets)*
Salt and freshly ground
black pepper
2 tsp olive oil

125g unsalted butter
3 tbsp capers in brine,
drained and washed
Zest and juice of ½ lemon
1 tbsp finely chopped parsley

METHOD – Season the trout fillets with salt and freshly ground black pepper. Heat the oil and 25g butter in a frying pan over a medium heat.

When the butter is foaming, add the trout fillets, skin-side down, hold them flat and cook for 2-3 minutes or until the skin is crisp and golden-brown and the flesh is almost cooked through.

Very carefully turn the trout fillets over and cook for a further minute. Transfer the fish carefully onto heated plates.

Add the remaining butter and the capers to the frying pan and cook until golden brown. Add the lemon zest and juice and parsley and season to taste. Spoon the butter over the trout and serve with a selection of vegetables.

Created by Jonathan Batchelor, Ramus

———

PAN FRIED SEA TROUT WITH PANCETTA

Serves Four

4 x 170g fillets of sea trout or
large rainbow trout
Salt & pepper
Juice of 1 lemon

1 tablespoon olive oil
30g butter
50g of pancetta cubed
8 spring onions, chopped
300ml dry white wine
Chopped parsley for garnish

METHOD – Season the sea trout with salt, black pepper and lemon juice. Heat the oil and butter in a frying pan and add the pancetta, fry for 2 to 3 minutes. Lower to medium heat and add the fish fillets and fry for 1 to 3 minutes per side.

Add the spring onions and the wine, bring to the boil and cook for 1 minute. Add a squeeze of lemon and serve the fish with new season potatoes.

TOP TIP – Add a knob of butter at the end to emulsify the sauce.

WINE MATCH – Sauvignon Blanc, Sancerre or
an oaked Chardonnay

Created by Jamie & Amy Roberts, Kilnsey Trout Farm

PAN-FRIED FILLET OF KILNSEY TROUT ON RATATOUILLE WITH CREAMY GOAT'S CHEESE

Serves Four

4 fresh trout fillets	4 courgettes
Olive oil and butter	2 garlic cloves
1 red onion	1 punnet cherry tomatoes
1 red pepper	½ bunch fresh basil
1 green pepper	1 tbsp tomato purée
½ aubergine	100ml full cream
	200g goat's cheese
	Salt and pepper and plain flour

METHOD – Dice the vegetables and add to a pan with a tablespoon of olive oil. Cook over a medium heat until the vegetables are turning golden. Add a tablespoon of tomato purée and some freshly chopped basil. Remove from the heat but keep warm.

Add the goat's cheese and cream to a saucepan. Cook over a low heat until the cheese is melted. Pass the mixture through a sieve. Put aside but keep hot.

Dust the trout fillets with flour seasoned with salt/pepper and pan fry with olive oil and butter. Turn the fillets half way through, allowing 3-4 minutes per side.

Assemble on warm plates.

Created by Jonathan Batchelor, Ramus

TUNA TARTARE

Serves Four as a Starter

300g finely diced fresh Sashimi
grade tuna
½ large red onion,
finely diced
1 dsp capers
50ml red wine vinegar

1 tsp Dijon mustard
4 green olives, diced
½ clove garlic, chopped
½ large green chilli, diced
50ml olive oil
½ lemon, squeezed
Salt and pepper

METHOD – Mix the onion, capers, vinegar, mustard, olives, garlic, chilli, lemon juice and olive oil in a bowl and season with salt and pepper.

Allow the mixture to sit for 10 to 15 minutes. At the last minute add the diced tuna and serve with or on crostini or Melba toast.

WINE MATCH – Chablis or Sauvignon Blanc

CHARGRILLED TUNA NIÇOISE

Serves Four

4 x 100gm steaks of yellowfin tuna loin
250g French beans, topped and tailed
250g small new potatoes
4 ripe tomatoes, skinned and quartered
4 eggs, hard boiled and halved
6 anchovy fillets

250g black olives
1 head of endive, yellow centre only

Dressing
1 tbsp red wine vinegar
1 tsp Dijon mustard
1 clove garlic, crushed
1 tbsp lemon juice & 6 tbsp olive oil

METHOD – Add the beans to boiling water, cook until tender, and then refresh in iced water. Cook the potatoes until tender, cool and then slice.

Heat a griddle pan or grill. Once hot, rub the tuna steaks in olive oil and black pepper and grill on both sides until cooked to your liking.

While the tuna is cooking, arrange the beans, potatoes, tomatoes, eggs, olives, anchovies & endive on a plate. Add the tuna and drizzle the vinaigrette over the salad.

FISH FACT

A yellowfin tuna can weigh up to 400kg and takes its name from the bright yellow fins running along the top and bottom side of the body.

WINE MATCH – New World Pinot Noir, Viognier or
any white grape from the Rhône area

OUR CATCH

40 of our most popular species

Images supplied by Seafish www.seafish.org

FISH FACT

The Guinness world record for the largest fish
and chips serving was made with a 22.65kg MSC
certified Norwegian line caught halibut.

Anchovy *(Engraulis encrasicolus)*

Appearance	Small, smooth, salty pinkish-brown fillets
Source	Mediterranean and Atlantic Ocean
Seasonality	Preserved fillets all year; best fresh Mar-Sep
How to Cook	Add, hot or cold, to salads, dips & sauces
Alternatives	Sardine, herring

Clam *(Veneridae)*

Appearance	Succulent, pale brown meat in a shell
Source	UK coastal waters
Seasonality	Best availability Sept-Apr; poor in summer
How to Cook	Steam; then grill or add to sauces & soups
Alternatives	Cockle, mussel

Cod *(Gadhus morhua)*

Appearance	Succulent, meaty, white flakes
Source	Sustainable MSC certified supplier
Seasonality	All year round; best quality Jul-Oct
How to Cook	Pan-fry, bake or poach
Alternatives	Haddock, coley, pollack, hake

Coley *(Pollachius virens)*

Appearance	Firm, white, meaty flakes
Source	North Sea; Atlantic Ocean
Seasonality	All year round; best quality Nov-Mar
How to Cook	Pan-fry, grill, bake or batter & deep-fry
Alternatives	Pollack, whiting, cod, haddock

Crab *(Cancer pagurus)*

Appearance	Brown body meat & white claw meat
Source	East & South coast of the UK
Seasonality	Feb-Oct; best quality Mar-Jun
How to Cook	Add to salads, tartlets, soups or sauces
Alternatives	Spider crab, snow crab, blue crab

Dover Sole *(Solea solea)*

Appearance	Velvet textured, firm, sweet, white flakes
Source	UK waters
Seasonality	Best availability in spring and autumn
How to Cook	Pan-fry, grill or poach simply
Alternatives	Lemon sole

Gurnard *(Aspitrigla cuculus)*

Appearance	Firm, pink, meaty flakes with robust flavour
Source	Various
Seasonality	Best availability May-Sept, poor in winter
How to Cook	Pan-fry, grill or stew; add to curries & soups
Alternatives	Red mullet, red snapper

Haddock *(Melanogrammas aeglefinus)*

Appearance	Sweet, succulent, meaty, white flakes
Source	Sustainable MSC certified supplier
Seasonality	All year round; best quality Feb-Sept
How to Cook	Pan-fry, grill, deep-fry, poach or bake
Alternatives	Cod, coley, pollack, hake

Halibut (Atlantic) *(Hippoglossus hippoglossus)*

Appearance	Large, meaty flakes with a velvet texture
Source	Farmed: Scottish Hebrides; wild: N. Atlantic
Seasonality	Farmed all year; wild season May-Mar
How to Cook	Pan-fry, grill, bake or poach simply
Alternatives	Turbot, brill

Hake *(Merluccius merluccius)*

Appearance	Soft, meaty, white flakes
Source	North Atlantic Ocean
Seasonality	Best availability May-Sept
How to Cook	Pan-fry, bake or poach
Alternatives	Cod, haddock, coley, pollack

Herring *(Clupea harengus)*

Appearance	Pale pink, delicate, oil-rich flesh
Source	North Atlantic
Seasonality	All year round; best quality Jun-Sept
How to Cook	Pan-fry, grill, poach or bake whole
Alternatives	Mackerel

John Dory *(Zeus faber)*

Appearance	Creamy white, firm, dense textured flesh
Source	East Atlantic and UK waters
Seasonality	Varied availability all year
How to Cook	Pan-fry, grill or bake whole
Alternatives	None - a unique species

Kipper *(Clupea harengus)*

Appearance	Plump, oil-rich, orange/brown flakes
Source	Swallowfish Ltd, Northumberland
Seasonality	All year round
How to Cook	Cover with boiling water, leave for 5 mins
Alternatives	Smoked haddock, Arbroath Smokies

Langoustine *(Nephrops norvegicus)*

Appearance	Firm, pinkish-white, segmented meat
Source	North Atlantic; North Sea
Seasonality	All year round; best quality Oct-Feb
How to Cook	Roast or boil; add meat to sauces/deep-fry
Alternatives	King prawn

Lemon Sole *(Microstomus kitt)*

Appearance	Small, soft, sweet tasting, white flakes
Source	UK coastal waters
Seasonality	All year round; best quality May-Mar
How to Cook	Pan-fry, grill, bake or poach
Alternatives	Dover sole, plaice

Lobster *(Nephropidae)*

Appearance	White, firm, meaty chunks from the tail
Source	Live: Nova Scotia, Canada & N. America
Seasonality	Available all year; best quality Apr-Nov
How to Cook	Grill or bake halved; add to sauces or soups
Alternatives	Crayfish, tiger prawn

Mackerel *(Scomber scombrus)*

Appearance	Delicious oil-rich flakes with strong flavour
Source	UK waters
Seasonality	All year; best quality in summer months
How to Cook	Grill or bake; smoked; in pâtés
Alternatives	Herring

Monkfish *(Lophius piscatorius)*

Appearance	Meaty texture, similar taste to langoustine
Source	Irish Sea, English Channel and North Sea
Seasonality	All year round; best quality Oct-May
How to Cook	Pan-fry, grill, bake, poach or steam
Alternatives	None

Mussel *(Mytulis edulis)*

Appearance	Pale pinkish-orange meat in a black shell
Source	Sustainable MSC certified from Shetland Isles
Seasonality	All year; best quality rope-grown Oct-Jul
How to Cook	Steam; add to sauces, pasta & rice dishes
Alternatives	Clam

Oyster *(Native – Ostrea edulis)*

Appearance	Soft, creamy coloured meat in an oval shell
Source	UK waters
Seasonality	Best quality Sept-Apr
How to Cook	Steam; top & grill or add to sauces
Alternatives	Mussel, clam, cockle

Plaice *(Pleuronectes platessa)*

Appearance	Very fine, delicate, white flakes
Source	North Atlantic fisheries
Seasonality	All year round; best quality May-Feb
How to Cook	Deep-fry, pan-fry, grill, bake or poach
Alternatives	Lemon sole, flounder, brill

Pollack *(Pollachius pollachius)*

Appearance	Firm, white flakes with a delicate flavour
Source	British & Irish coastal waters
Seasonality	All year round; best quality Nov-May
How to Cook	Batter & deep-fry, pan-fry, grill or poach
Alternatives	Cod, haddock, coley

Rainbow Trout *(Oncorhynchus mykiss)*

Appearance	Small, delicate, oil-rich, pale pink flakes
Source	Farmed at Kilnsey, North Yorkshire
Seasonality	Available all year round
How to Cook	Pan-fry, grill or bake; eat hot, cold or smoked
Alternatives	Brown trout, sea trout, salmon

Red Mullet *(Mullus barbatus)*

Appearance	Soft, pale pink flesh with shellfish flavour
Source	From South Coast
Seasonality	Best quality Aug-Oct
How to Cook	Pan-fry, grill, steam or bake whole
Alternatives	Red snapper

Red Snapper *(Lutjanus sanguine)*

Appearance	Delicate pale pink flakes with strong flavour
Source	Various
Seasonality	All year round; best availability Mar-Sept
How to Cook	Pan-fry, grill or bake/barbecue whole
Alternatives	Red mullet, other varieties of snapper

Salmon *(Salmo salar)*

Appearance	Large, oil rich, pinkish-orange flakes
Source	Wild - Scottish rivers; farmed - Wester Ross
Seasonality	Farmed all year; wild season Apr-Sept
How to Cook	Pan-fry, grill, bake, poach – eat hot or cold
Alternatives	Sea trout, rainbow trout, pacific salmon

Sardine *(Sardina pilchardus)*

Appearance	Small, silver fish with dark, oily flesh
Source	UK south coast; Mediterranean waters
Seasonality	All year round; best quality Oct-May
How to Cook	Grill or barbecue whole
Alternatives	Herring

Scallop *(Pecten maximus)*

Appearance	Firm, white, succulent meat with orange roe
Source	Cool Scottish waters
Seasonality	All year round; best quality Mar-Nov
How to Cook	Pan-fry out of shell; steam/grill within shells
Alternatives	Peeled prawns, razor clams

Scarborough Woof *(Anarhichas lupus)*

Appearance	Cod-like, firm, white, succulent flakes
Source	North Atlantic, North Sea
Seasonality	Best availability Apr-Oct
How to Cook	Pan-fry, grill, bake, poach or batter/deep-fry
Alternatives	Cod, haddock

Sea Bass *(Dicentrarchus labrax)*

Appearance	Small, sweet, white flakes with a firm texture
Source	Farmed - Mediterranean; wild – UK waters
Seasonality	Farmed all year; wild season Aug-Mar
How to Cook	Pan-fry, grill, poach or bake whole
Alternatives	Sea (gilthead) bream

Sea Bream (Gilthead) *(Sparus aurata)*

Appearance	Firm, succulent, opaque, pinkish flesh
Source	English Channel (wild); the Med (farmed)
Seasonality	Farmed all year; best quality May-Jul
How to Cook	Pan-fry, grill, poach or bake whole
Alternatives	Snapper, sea bass

Sea Trout *(Salmo trutta)*

Appearance	Pale pink, sweet, oil rich flesh
Source	Wild sea trout - caught from Scottish Rivers
Seasonality	All year round; best quality May-Aug
How to Cook	Pan-fry, grill, bake or poach
Alternatives	Rainbow trout, salmon

Skate *(Rajidae family)*

Appearance	Firm, pinkish-brown, meaty 'wings'
Source	UK waters
Seasonality	Best availability Jun-Oct
How to Cook	Pan-fry, bake or poach
Alternatives	Ray

Smoked Haddock *(Melanogrammas aeglefinus)*

Appearance	Succulent, meaty, white fillets tinged yellow
Source	Grimsby smoked (PGI status)
Seasonality	All year round
How to Cook	Cover with boiling water, leave for 2 mins
Alternatives	None

Squid *(Loligo vulgaris)*

Appearance	Firm, cream-coloured body & tentacles
Source	UK waters
Seasonality	All year round; best quality Oct-Mar
How to Cook	Pan-fry, grill or batter & deep-fry
Alternatives	Cuttlefish, octopus

Swordfish *(Xiphias gladius)*

Appearance	Firm, succulent white & dark (red) meat
Source	Sustainable MSC certified fisheries
Seasonality	Best quality Apr-Dec
How to Cook	Pan-fry, grill, bake, barbecue or stew
Alternatives	Tuna

Tiger Prawn *(Penaeus monodon)*

Appearance	Semi-transparent meat encased in a shell
Source	Indian Ocean
Seasonality	All year round
How to Cook	Pan-fry, grill, barbecue and add to sauces
Alternatives	Lobster

Turbot *(Psetta maxima)*

Appearance	Firm textured, white flakes with strong flavour
Source	Farmed: Spain & Norway; wild: South coast
Seasonality	All year round; wild season Apr-Feb
How to Cook	Pan-fry, grill, bake, poach or steam
Alternatives	Atlantic halibut, brill

Whiting *(Merlangius merlangus)*

Appearance	Firm, white, meaty flakes
Source	North Sea; Atlantic Ocean
Seasonality	All year round; best quality Oct-Mar
How to Cook	Pan-fry, grill, bake, poach or deep-fry
Alternatives	Cod, haddock, coley, pollack

Yellowfin Tuna *(Thunnus ibacor)*

Appearance	Firm, dark pink, meaty steaks
Source	Pacific & Indian Oceans (dolphin-friendly)
Seasonality	All year round
How to Cook	Best seared like a steak or grilled
Alternatives	Marlin, swordfish

CONTRIBUTORS

Achieving longevity in business only happens with a lot of hard work and commitment, and the forty years of Ramus Seafoods have come about with perhaps more than most.

With that in mind I would like to thank our great team, both past and present, who have put in so much effort, our fabulous suppliers for all the great fish, our fantastic customers who continue to support us and of course Chris & Liz Ramus for their vision, dedication and sacrifice.

I would also like to thank Simon Hylton *(Photography)*, Nick Rayner, Emily Bennison, Daniel Holmes *(Graphic Design)*, Liam Gill and all of our recipe contributors for helping me to realise the long held ambition of a Ramus cookery book.

Jonathan Batchelor, MD Ramus Seafoods

VISIT RAMUS
www.ramus.co.uk

Harrogate store:
136 Kings Road,
Harrogate, HG1 5HY

01423 563271

Ilkley store:
2 South Hawksworth Street,
Ilkley, LS29 9DX

01943 600388